TABLE OF CONTENT

INTRODUCTION

This book delves into the convergence of Human Resource Management strategies, policies, and practices with the concept of environmental sustainability in light of climate change, environmental deterioration, and the pressing need for sustainable practices. The book underscores the notion of "Green HRM" as a promising and transformative idea, seeking to reinvent our approach to human resources within the framework of environmental sustainability.

Chapter 1: The Emergence of Green Human Resource Management

The book explores the origins of Green HRM, its evolution in response to environmental challenges, and the historical context of its integration. It delves into the milestones and paradigm shifts that have shaped the integration of green principles into HRM practices, from early sustainability movements to global environmental concerns, providing a foundation for understanding its necessity and urgency.

Chapter 2: Understanding Green HRM

This book provides a comprehensive understanding of Green HRM, covering its principles and components, from sustainable HR policies to eco-friendly training and development initiatives. It uses case studies and real-world examples to illustrate how organizations can align their HR strategies with environmental sustainability, paving the way for meaningful change.

Chapter 3: The Argument for Green HRM in Business

This chapter explores the business case for Green HRM, highlighting its numerous benefits such as cost savings, enhanced corporate reputation, and increased employee engagement. It uses empirical evidence and industry best practices to argue that Green HRM is not only a moral imperative but also a strategic advantage in the competitive landscape.

Chapter 4: Green Recruitment and Selection

Chapter 4 discusses the application of Green HRM principles in the recruitment and selection process, offering practical insights into building a workforce aligned with sustainability goals. It provides real-world case studies of organizations successfully integrating green practices into their hiring processes, emphasizing the importance of environmental awareness in talent selection.

Chapter 5: Sustainable Employee Engagement

Chapter 5 discusses the role of Green HRM in promoting sustainable engagement among employees. It discusses initiatives like wellness programs, sustainability training, and team-building activities. These initiatives foster a culture of sustainability, empowering employees to advocate for positive change within and outside the company.

Chapter 6: Green Training and Development

Chapter 6 discusses the application of Green HRM in training and development initiatives, focusing on eco-friendly programs, technology use to reduce learning's carbon footprint, and sustainability principles in leadership development. It highlights how organizations can cultivate a workforce capable of driving sustainable change through practical examples.

Chapter 7: Sustainable Performance Management

Chapter 7 discusses the role of Green HRM in enhancing performance management by aligning employee goals with organizational objectives. It discusses the integration of sustainability metrics into performance evaluations, feedback's role in promoting eco-conscious behaviors, and setting sustainability-related goals. Real-world case studies demonstrate how sustainable performance management can drive progress.

Chapter 8: Green Compensation and Benefit

Chapter 8 explores the application of Green HRM in compensation and benefits structures, focusing on eco-friendly compensation packages, sustainable incentive programs, and green perks for attracting and retaining top talent, thereby motivating employees to contribute to environmental goals.

Chapter 9: Green Workplace Culture

Chapter 9 explores the importance of organizational culture in shaping employee behavior and attitudes. It highlights the role of leadership in promoting environmental consciousness, the significance of communication in fostering sustainability culture, and the integration of green values into an organization's mission and vision. Case studies are used to illustrate successful green workplace cultures.

Chapter 10: Overcoming Challenges and Future Trends

The chapter discusses the challenges and future trends of Green HRM, highlighting potential obstacles such as resistance to change and environmental impact measurement complexities. It also highlights emerging trends like artificial intelligence, blockchain, and big data analytics, providing insights for organizations to overcome these challenges and stay at the forefront of eco-conscious HR practices.

CHAPTER 1: THE EMERGENCE OF GREEN HUMAN RESOURCE MANAGEMENT

The rise of Green Human Resource Management (Green HRM) may be situated within the historical progression of growing environmental consciousness and sustainability considerations that have had a substantial influence on the worldwide corporate environment. Over the last few decades, there has been an increasing acknowledgement of environmental issues, including climate change, depletion of resources, and loss of biodiversity. As a result, organizations have been prompted to reassess their operating strategy. In light of the pressing environmental concerns, the concept of Green HRM has emerged as a strategy framework aimed at integrating human resource practices with sustainability goals.

The change observed in human resource management (HRM) techniques may be seen as a manifestation of larger societal trends towards sustainability and corporate social responsibility (CSR). It has been recognized by organizations that in order to maintain competitiveness and responsibility, they must include environmental sustainability into their fundamental operations, which includes human resources activities. The objective of Green HRM is to encourage environmentally friendly behaviors among employees, foster an organizational culture that is mindful of the environment, and include sustainability into several HR activities, including recruiting, training, and performance monitoring.

Moreover, the significance of Green HRM as a reaction to environmental challenges is further emphasized by its historical background. There is a growing recognition among organizations of the need of showcasing their dedication to environmental stewardship, not just in the realm of their offerings and operations, but also in their approach to managing their employees. The historical context presented emphasizes the rise of Green HRM as a crucial mechanism for promoting environmental responsibility and social consciousness inside enterprises' human resource management strategies. This, in turn, contributes to the overarching objective of achieving sustainable development.

The Origin of Green HRM

The concept of Green HRM emerged as a result of the intersection of environmental consciousness, corporate social responsibility (CSR), and developing business strategies. The emergence of this phenomenon may be attributed to the increasing acknowledgement of environmental issues and the necessity for companies to include sustainable strategies. The environmental movement that emerged in the 20th century effectively heightened public consciousness about concerns such as pollution and climate change, therefore compelling corporations to contemplate their ecological footprint. Concurrently, the notion of CSR gained significance, underscoring the significance of firms' societal contributions, including environmental stewardship. The need for comprehensive sustainability measures is further emphasized by sustainability reporting and international standards such as ISO 14001. With the increasing prevalence of green business practices and marketing techniques, it became necessary for HR departments to ensure alignment of their policies with the company's environmentally conscious image. The development of Green HRM was influenced significantly by academic research, regulatory concerns, and the integration of sustainability principles into supply chain management. Currently, Green HRM is regarded as a strategic strategy that incorporates concepts of environmental sustainability into different HR responsibilities, hence promoting awareness and implementation of sustainable practices across the whole employment lifecycle.

Milestones and Paradigm Shifts

As the passage of time unfolds, we are confronted with notable landmarks and transformative events that have influenced the incorporation of environmentally conscious ideas into human resource management (HRM) procedures.

1. Sustainability Movements

The 1970s witnessed the rise of the contemporary environmental movement. The emergence of Earth Day in 1970 was a significant milestone, serving as a symbolic catalyst that mobilized a vast number of individuals to express their apprehensions over the deterioration of the environment. The incident served as a catalyst for corporations to acknowledge their responsibility in the conservation of the environment. The concept of sustainability emerged as global awareness grew on the significance of conscientious management of the Earth.

2. Legislation and Regulation

In the latter part of the twentieth century, significant environmental laws was implemented. The United States, as an example, implemented significant legislative measures such as the Clean Air Act and the Clean Water Act. These regulatory frameworks have imposed a legal requirement on organizations to adopt environmentally friendly activities, rather than leaving it as a discretionary matter. The growing regulatory landscape necessitated that firms adjust, leading to compliance being a significant concern for HRM.

3. Globalization of Environmental Concerns

The latter half of the 20th century and the early part of the 21st century witnessed the advent of the globalized discourse surrounding environmental issues. There has been a notable global transformation as environmental concerns have surpassed the confines of individual nations. Climate change, deforestation, resource shortages, and pollution have emerged as global concerns with wide-reaching impacts on a global scale, affecting individuals and communities worldwide. Organizations functioning in a global setting have come to recognize that sustainability is not only a local matter, but rather a worldwide one. The adoption of a global viewpoint has led to a more holistic approach to sustainability within the field of HRM.

The Necessity and Urgency of Green HRM

In the present day, as we grapple with more severe environmental challenges, the imperative and immediacy of Green Human Resource Management (HRM) have become more evident than ever before. Climate change, biodiversity loss, and the depletion of finite resources are not only conceptual issues; rather, they represent pressing and fundamental challenges that require urgent attention and action.

HRM has arisen as a direct reaction to the aforementioned difficulties. The statement acknowledges the notion that employees are not only components inside the operational framework of an organization, but rather, they play a pivotal role as active participants in the firm's endeavors towards achieving sustainability. By integrating human resource practices with environmentally conscious ideas, firms have the potential to substantially diminish their ecological impact while simultaneously leveraging the combined efforts of their employees to propel sustainability endeavors.

Green HRM as a Strategic Imperative

The notion of Green HRM has transitioned from being a niche idea or a peripheral endeavor to being a strategic necessity for enterprises. In a contemporary context where the preservation of the environment is of utmost importance, stakeholders, including consumers, investors, and regulators, are placing greater emphasis on evaluating an organization's sustainability initiatives. In this regard, Green HRM emerges as a potent mechanism for sustaining competitiveness and ensuring continued relevance.

Greening the Workforce

The integration of green principles into HRM practices involves several key aspects:

1. Recruitment and Talent Acquisition

There is a growing trend among contemporary job candidates to prioritize environmental consciousness. Individuals actively search for companies whose values are congruent with their own, and they exhibit a preference for firms that promote the concept of sustainability. Green HRM acknowledges the aforementioned change in priorities and proactively advocates for an organization's environmental credentials in order to recruit highly skilled individuals.

2. Employee Engagement and Development

The involvement of employees in sustainability efforts not only harnesses their skills and creativity, but also cultivates a feeling of purpose. Employees who perceive that their work is aligned with a broader and significant objective, such as the preservation of the environment, are inclined to exhibit higher levels of motivation, job satisfaction, and organizational commitment.

3. Training and Development

Green HRM emphasizes the need of incorporating environmental education and training into organizational practices. The program guarantees that staff possess the necessary knowledge and abilities to effectively incorporate sustainable practices into their regular work activities. The training encompasses several aspects such as energy saving, waste reduction, sustainable sourcing, and other environmentally conscious efforts.

4. Sustainability Metrics and Reporting

As firms increasingly prioritize sustainability objectives, the implementation of Green HRM assumes a crucial function in monitoring and communicating advancements towards these goals. Metrics pertaining to employee participation in sustainability initiatives, conservation of resources, and mitigation of carbon emissions assume a critical role in substantiating an organization's dedication to environmentally conscious goals.

Summary

The investigation of Green HRM reveals that its inception and development have been motivated by a growing recognition of the ecological issues confronting our global society. The evolution of Green HRM, from its inception in early sustainability movements to its current state of globalized environmental concerns, serves as a monument to the changing priorities of both society and companies.

In the subsequent chapters, a more comprehensive exploration of the pragmatic dimensions of Green HRM will be undertaken, with a particular focus on its effects on businesses, employees, and the wider societal context. This study aims to examine the impact of Green HRM on organizational sustainability, with a focus on its potential to drive environmental responsibility and contribute to a sustainable future.

CHAPTER 2: UNDERSTANDING GREEN HRM

The comprehension and interpretation of a given subject matter. Green HRM, also known as Green HRM, is a modern approach in the realm of human resource management that emphasizes the incorporation of environmental sustainability concepts into various HR practices and initiatives. The concept of Green HRM acknowledges that firms bear a duty to effectively manage their human resources in a manner that is consistent with overarching objectives of environmental sustainability. This idea incorporates a range of human resources tasks and practices, including as recruiting, training, performance management, and employee engagement, all with the objective of cultivating a sustainable and environmentally conscious company culture.

One of the fundamental principles behind Green HRM is the recognition of employees as pivotal contributors to an organization's endeavors towards sustainability. Therefore, it is important for human resources professionals to actively participate in the development of the organization's sustainability strategy and to guarantee that employees are fully engaged and well-informed on sustainability activities.

DEFINING GREEN HRM

"Green HRM involves the use of HRM policies and practices to promote the sustainable use of human and social capital in ways that minimize environmental harm and maximize social good."

(Renwick, D. W., et al., 2013)

Green HRM refers to a strategy framework that incorporates environmental sustainability concepts into the various human resource practices and policies used by enterprises. The primary objective of this initiative is to actively encourage the principles of sustainability, mitigate adverse effects on the environment, and cultivate a societal mindset that prioritizes ecological awareness. Green HRM is a strategic approach that aims to integrate human resource strategies with an organization's sustainability objectives. This approach recognizes the interconnectedness between a sustainable environment and the achievement of business goals. The statement acknowledges the significant contribution of employees in promoting sustainability objectives and aims to harmonize human resources policies with an organization's environmental goals. Green HRM is a strategic approach that aims to address the increasing recognition of environmental concerns and the imperative for organizations to play a role in fostering a sustainable future. The concept of Green HRM acknowledges the significant contribution of employees towards the achievement of sustainability objectives and aims to harmonize human resource practices with an organization's dedication to environmental stewardship. The primary objective of Green HRM is to promote a sustainable future by emphasizing environmentally responsible behavior among employees.

Key Principles of Green HRM

Green HRM is a conceptual framework that seeks to harmonize an organization's human resource practices with its objectives in environmental sustainability. The focal point is in the incorporation of environmental factors into several human resources activities and initiatives. Green HRM is founded upon a number of fundamental concepts that establish a structure for harmonizing HR activities with an organization's dedication to environmental accountability. These concepts are the fundamental basis for establishing a workforce that is both sustainable and ecologically responsible. Green human resource management (HRM) is firmly rooted in scholarly research and pragmatic observations, offering a structured approach for incorporating environmental factors into HR practices and initiatives. By integrating these ideas, firms have the ability to cultivate a workforce that is more sustainable and ecologically conscious, therefore showcasing their dedication to environmental responsibility.

Environmental Awareness and Education: The implementation of Green HRM commences by fostering environmental consciousness among employees and providing them with education on the environmental policies and practices of the firm. This facilitates the development of a labor force that comprehends the significance of sustainability. Green HRM is predicated on the fundamental ideas of environmental consciousness and knowledge dissemination as fundamental components for cultivating sustainability inside enterprises. The initial premise of environmental awareness underscores the development of a profound comprehension of environmental issues and the significance of implementing sustainable practices among both employees and stakeholders. The recognition of this knowledge plays a crucial role in stimulating individuals to actively participate in environmentally friendly endeavors.

Eco-friendly Recruitment and Selection: The Human Resources (HR) department has significant potential in the recruitment process of personnel who possess a strong environmental awareness and exhibit the necessary competencies and drive to actively participate in sustainable endeavors inside the firm. The recruiting and selection process in Green HRM involves firms actively seeking people who possess the necessary skills and also demonstrate alignment with the company's environmental principles. This may entail evaluating a candidate's level of environmental awareness or previous engagement in sustainable undertakings. Green HRM is the process of not only considering candidates' credentials but also evaluating their compatibility with the organization's environmental principles and objectives related to sustainability. This may entail evaluating a candidate's level of knowledge and dedication towards environmental concerns.

Training and Development: Sustainability training and development may help employees adopt green work practices. Green HRM stresses sustainability training and development. Companies teach staff about environmental concerns, eco-friendly practices, and sustainability goals. This lets employees help the environment. Green HRM companies provide sustainability training to staff. This encourages employees to promote environmental goals. Eco-friendly recruiting and selection are core elements of Green HRM. This philosophy stresses incorporating environmental factors into hiring. As companies prioritize sustainability, hiring people who have the abilities and share their environmental values is vital.

Performance Management: Green HRM places emphasis on the evaluation, recognition, and enhancement of employees' environmental sustainability endeavors via performance management. The assumption is made that the inclusion of employees is essential for the achievement of sustainability goals, and that their performance should be evaluated based on environmentally friendly standards. According to Delmas & Montes-Sancho, (2011), it is recommended that performance management include sustainability indicators like as energy efficiency, waste reduction, and environmental compliance, in addition to job-related metrics. According to Renwick et al. (2013), the implementation of performance management within the context of green HRM serves to foster sustainable accountability and responsibility. The performance of staff members is evaluated based on their fulfillment of job responsibilities as well as their contributions to the environment. This initiative fosters the principles of sustainability and motivates employees to adopt environmentally-friendly practices.

Green Policies and Practices: Green HR strategies including paper reduction, telecommuting, and energy-efficient technology may reduce an organization's environmental effect. Green HRM involves integrating green policies and practices into an organization's HR procedures. It emphasizes the need to incorporate environmental sustainability into human resources policy and practices. This entails creating and executing HR policies that reflect an organization's sustainability and environmental responsibilities. Sustainable HR strategies are based on policies and practices, which shape organizational culture and employee behavior. These green policies and practices include recruiting, training, performance management, remuneration, and employee engagement. Green recruiting practices may stress employing people who share the company's environmental ideals and commitment.

Performance Evaluation: The evaluation of employee performance within the context of Green HRM often includes the assessment of their contributions towards achieving sustainability objectives. Performance evaluations may include metrics pertaining to energy saving, trash reduction, and several other environmental indicators. Performance management plays a crucial role in the implementation of Green HRM, as it facilitates the integration of an organization's sustainability objectives with the performance of individuals and teams. This concept acknowledges the potential of good performance management to foster environmentally responsible behavior and results among employees. The process encompasses several essential elements, such as the formulation of precise environmental performance indicators and the incorporation of sustainability objectives into performance assessments. These measures may include energy conservation, waste reduction, carbon footprint, and several other environmental indicators.

Employee Engagement: Employee participation in environmental activities and decision-making may increase morale and sustainability objectives. Green HRM engages employees in sustainability efforts. Regular communication channels educate employees about the company's environmental successes and difficulties. Involve all staff in sustainability decisions and projects.

Green HRM stresses employee participation in environmental sustainability activities. This concept recognizes that employee participation is crucial to achieving sustainability objectives and implementing eco-friendly practices. Green HRM encourages employees to take ownership of sustainability. Green HRM emphasizes employee participation in environmental sustainability activities. This concept emphasizes that green policies and practices need an engaged and motivated workforce. Research shows that engaged employees promote eco-friendly behaviours, improving environmental performance.

Employee Engagement and Communication: Green human resource management (HRM) promotes employee engagement via the active participation of employees in sustainability efforts. The firm has established regular communication channels to effectively disseminate information to employees on its environmental accomplishments and obstacles. Employee engagement and communication are essential tenets of Green HRM, emphasizing the significance of employee involvement in environmental sustainability projects and the promotion of open and transparent communication channels. This concept recognizes the significance of a committed staff in effectively implementing environmentally sustainable policies and practices within organizational settings. According to R. Schuler & E. Jackson, (2014), empirical studies have shown that employees who actively participate in sustainability initiatives tend to adopt and promote eco-conscious behaviors, hence contributing to enhanced environmental performance. Employee involvement and effective communication are fundamental aspects of Green HRM that play a crucial role in promoting environmental sustainability inside firms. This concept acknowledges the significance of a committed staff that is well-informed about sustainability objectives and accomplishments, as it serves as a crucial catalyst for promoting environmentally aware behaviors and endorsing environmental endeavors. The significance of including employees in sustainability initiatives is highlighted by research, as it results in enhanced environmental performance and a stronger dedication to eco-friendly behaviors.

Green Leadership Development: Leaders and managers assume a crucial role in the implementation of environmentally sustainable projects. Green HRM is a strategic approach that focuses on the identification and cultivation of leadership skills pertaining to sustainability. It aims to foster responsible decision-making and the adoption of environmentally friendly practices across all organizational levels. Green HRM emphasizes the central premise of green leadership development as an essential element in promoting environmental sustainability inside enterprises. This concept acknowledges the significant impact that strong leadership has on driving and advocating for sustainability efforts.

Compensation and Incentives: In order to encourage staff to meet sustainability objectives, organizations might establish incentive systems. In order to incentivize employees to actively contribute towards environmental goals, many measures may be used, such as the provision of cash incentives, more time off, or other supplementary benefits. Compensation and incentives are fundamental ideas within the framework of Green HRM, emphasizing the significance of providing rewards and motivation to employees in order to foster their active engagement in an organization's pursuit of environmental sustainability objectives. This theory recognizes that both monetary and non-monetary incentives may be effective means of encouraging environmentally responsible actions and cultivating a sustainable mindset among employees. Organizations often develop remuneration packages and incentives that aim to motivate employees in attaining sustainability objectives and adopting environmentally responsible behaviors, but with potential variations in particular practices.

Green Supply Chain Management: Green HRM encompasses activities that transcend the confines of a company, as it engages in collaborative efforts with suppliers and partners to foster sustainable practices throughout the whole supply chain. Human resources (HR) may assume a significant role in the process of choosing environmentally conscious suppliers and overseeing their adherence to sustainability criteria. Green HRM expands its impact beyond the confines of a company by placing a strong emphasis on green supply chain management as a core tenet. This notion acknowledges that the environmental influence of a corporation is not confined just to its internal activities, but rather encompasses its whole supply chain. Green HRM places significant emphasis on the collaborative efforts of organizations and their suppliers and partners to uphold sustainable practices throughout the whole supply chain. The adherence to environmentally conscious supply chain management practices is crucial in attaining an organization's sustainability objectives.

Reporting and Compliance: Green HRM plays a crucial role in the collection and dissemination of information pertaining to environmental performance (EP). By doing so, it ensures that the company adheres to environmental rules and fulfills sustainability reporting obligations. The concepts of reporting and compliance play a crucial role in Green HRM, highlighting the need of precise environmental reporting and adherence to sustainability standards and laws. The aforementioned concept acknowledges the significance of openness and accountability in evaluating and enhancing an organization's environmental performance (OEP). Furthermore, this perspective is in line with the increasing international emphasis on sustainability reporting and the need to adhere to environmental legislation and regulations.

Employee Well-being and Health: Green HRM is a strategic approach that encompasses the consideration of employee's health and well-being within the framework of environmental sustainability. The implementation of measures such as establishing a secure and environmentally conscious work environment, providing wellness initiatives, and advocating for a harmonious equilibrium between work and personal life may be considered. The core tenet of Green HRM is on prioritizing the welfare and physical condition of employees within the framework of environmental sustainability. The aforementioned concept acknowledges the significance of employee health and well-being in the pursuit of sustainability goals, emphasizing that a workforce in good health is more inclined to actively participate in environmentally responsible behaviors. According to Renwick et al. (2013), there is a scholarly discourse around the notion that a sustainable workplace encompasses the integration of factors pertaining to the physical and psychological well-being of employees, with the establishment of an environmentally conscious work environment.

Change Management: The successful implementation of Green HRM often necessitates organizational modifications. Human resource professionals have a vital role in effectively managing these organizational changes, therefore ensuring that staff are fully engaged and aligned with sustainability goals, while also successfully adjusting to novel methods. Change management is an essential concept in the field of Green Human Resource Management (Green HRM), which acknowledges the need of proficiently directing and executing environmental sustainability activities within organizational settings. This concept recognizes that the transition towards adopting more environmentally aware activities often necessitates substantial organizational modifications, including adjustments in procedures, frameworks, and cultural norms. According to Renwick, Redman, and Maguire (2013), the implementation of Green HRM is crucial in successfully managing organizational transformations and guaranteeing the efficient achievement of sustainability objectives.

Significance of Green HRM

Green HRM holds significant importance in today's business landscape for several reasons:

Sustainability: Assisting firms in aligning their human resources (HR) practices with their sustainability objectives is crucial in fostering a future characterized by sustainability and responsibility.

Cost Efficiency: Through the reduction of resource consumption and the optimization of operations, the implementation of Green HRM has the potential to provide cost savings and enhance financial performance.

Compliance and Risk Management: The implementation of environmental legislation ensures that firms maintain compliance and effectively manage the potential consequences associated with non-compliance in environmental matters.

Employee Engagement: Employees that are actively involved and possess a strong environmental awareness are more inclined to make good contributions towards the sustainability initiatives of the firm.

Reputation Building: The use of Green HRM practices has the potential to bolster an organization's standing as an ecologically conscientious institution, hence appealing to stakeholders that emphasize sustainability.

CHAPTER 3: THE BUSINESS CASE FOR GREEN HRM

In a time characterized by pressing environmental issues and increased consciousness of sustainability, Green HRM emerges as a paradigm-shifting methodology that surpasses mere altruistic intentions. The alignment of HR practices with environmental sustainability is considered a strategic necessity due to its potential to provide competitive advantage and enhance corporate resilience.

The Compelling Business Case for Green HRM

1. Cost Savings and Efficiency

Implementing environmentally aware human resources (HR) practices has the potential to result in significant cost savings. Strategies such as the reduction of paper consumption, the adoption of energy-efficient procedures, and the encouragement of remote work have the potential to result in decreased operating costs, hence exerting a favorable influence on financial performance.

2. Enhanced Corporate Reputation

The implementation of Green human resource management practices contributes to the enhancement of an organization's reputation as a socially responsible and sustainable employer. The establishment of such a reputation has the potential to foster heightened levels of consumer loyalty, trust, and a distinct competitive advantage inside the market.

3. Employee Engagement and Retention

Green HRM promotes the establishment of a sustainable culture within the organizational setting. When employees perceive that their firm aligns with their environmental values and demonstrates a proactive commitment to sustainability, it enhances their level of engagement and job satisfaction, hence mitigating turnover rates.

4. Compliance and Risk Mitigation

Green HRM is a strategic approach that aims to guarantee organizational compliance with environmental laws and regulations, hence mitigating legal risks and possible financial penalties. The methodology offers a systematic approach to proactively manage and mitigate compliance risks.

5. Innovation and Competitive Advantage

Green HRM promotes the active involvement of employees in proposing and executing sustainability projects. This phenomenon has the potential to result in the development of novel goods, procedures, and cost-effective strategies, therefore conferring a competitive edge within the marketplace.

6. Long-Term Sustainability

By incorporating sustainability principles into their human resources (HR) strategies, firms enhance their capacity to withstand environmental disturbances and effectively adapt to evolving business environments. Green HRM is a strategic approach that aims to integrate sustainability principles into the organizational culture, so ensuring the long-term viability and durability of the business.

7. Stakeholder Engagement

The use of Green HRM practices signifies a dedication to the principles of sustainability, fostering stronger connections with many stakeholders, and appealing to investors that prioritize social responsibility.

Case Study: Patagonia's Approach to Green HRM

Organizational Context: Patagonia, the renowned firm specializing in outdoor clothing and gear, has gained considerable recognition due to its pioneering efforts in the realm of sustainability. This case study investigates the distinctive "Pay-for-Sustainability" model used by Patagonia, which prioritizes environmental and social responsibility. It demonstrates how this strategy is consistent with the company's principles and contributes to the achievement of corporate objectives as well as sustainability targets.

The Sustainable Approach to Patagonia

Since its establishment, Patagonia has shown a robust dedication to both environmental and social responsibility. The founder, Yvon Chouinard, had a goal of establishing a firm that not only manufactured items of superior quality, but also prioritized the reduction of its environmental impact and the promotion of ethical business practices.

Green HRM Initiatives:

1. **Eco-Friendly Employee Benefits:** Patagonia provides many perks, including remunerated leave for engaging in environmental volunteer work and rewards for practicing carpooling or using public transit.

2. **Sustainability Training:** The organization provides its employees with access to training programs focused on sustainability, which aim to educate them on environmental concerns and Patagonia's objective.

3. **Eco-Focused Recruitment:** Patagonia engages in proactive recruitment efforts to attract employees that possess a deep commitment to environmental causes, therefore ensuring that their staff is in harmony with the company's overarching sustainability objectives.

Results: The implementation of Green HRM by Patagonia has not only resulted in an improved perception of the company as an ecologically responsible employer, but has also had a positive impact on employee engagement and retention. The company's unwavering emphasis on sustainability garners positive reception from both consumers and investors, so bolstering its ongoing prosperity.

Summary

The rationale for implementing Green HRM is clear and persuasive. The provision of a wide range of advantages is seen, which have a favorable influence on an organization's financial outcomes, reputation, level of employee involvement, and overall capacity for long-term viability. Organizations that adopt eco-conscious human resources strategies not only demonstrate alignment with the increasing environmental awareness of stakeholders but also get a strategic edge within the competitive business climate. The implementation of Green HRM is not just driven by moral obligations, but rather serves as a means to foster resilience, responsibility, and prosperity within the corporate sphere.

CHAPTER 4: GREEN RECRUITMENT AND SELECTION

Recruitment and selection are essential human resource responsibilities that significantly impact an organization's capacity to achieve its sustainability goals. The concept of Green HRM extends beyond conventional talent acquisition practices, since it aims to identify employees who not only possess the necessary skills but also demonstrate a shared dedication to environmental sustainability inside the firm.

Identifying Environmentally Conscious Candidates

1. Green Job Postings

The first stage of green recruiting involves the formulation of employment advertisements that emphasize the organization's dedication to sustainability. Terms such as "environmentally responsible," "sustainability-driven," or "eco-conscious" may appeal to those who possess a strong inclination towards environmental concerns.

2. Eco-conscious Screening

In the preliminary evaluation phase, the human resources department has the opportunity to include inquiries pertaining to sustainability. The replies of the candidates provide valuable insights on their level of environmental consciousness and the importance they place on environmental principles.

3. Sustainable Sourcing

The use of job boards and recruiting platforms that specifically target job searchers with a strong environmental consciousness may effectively expedite the process of locating candidates that align with the organization's sustainability objectives.

Eco-friendly Interviewing Practices

1. Virtual Interviews

One of the most direct methods for aligning interviews with environmentally conscious ideas is by conducting them in a virtual format. This practice effectively mitigates the environmental consequences linked to transportation, while fostering enhanced efficiency.

2. Sustainable Interview Locations

Choosing interview locations that comply with green building standards or have convenient access to public transit supports the organization's commitment to environmental sustainability.

3. Sustainable Materials

The act of providing candidates with materials composed of recycled or sustainable resources, such as brochures and presentation slides, serves as a concrete manifestation of a dedicated adherence to sustainability principles.

Case Study 1: Google's Sustainable Hiring Practices

Organizational Context: Google, a prominent multinational technology campany, is well recognized for its exceptional levels of innovation and industry leadership within the technology sector. In addition to its notable scientific achievements, the firm has garnered acclaim for its steadfast dedication to sustainability.

Green Recruitment Initiatives:

1. **Green Job Postings:** The job ads of Google prominently emphasize the company's dedication to sustainability and environmental stewardship. The firm places significant emphasis on its ambitious environmental objectives and its unwavering commitment to effecting a beneficial influence.

2. **Eco-conscious Screening:** During the interview process, Google evaluates applicants' level of conformity to its sustainability principles. The interview process includes inquiries pertaining to environmental responsibility in order to discern applicants that align with the organization's ecological goals.

Results: The use of environmentally conscious recruiting strategies by Google has facilitated the company's capacity to attract individuals who possess a strong dedication to sustainability. The congruence of values has played a significant role in the achievements of Google's environmentally aware endeavors and has enhanced its standing as a preferred employer with a commitment to sustainability.

Case Study 2: IKEA's Sustainable Interview Locations

Organizational Context: IKEA, the Swedish multinational furniture retailer, is recognized not only for its affordable and stylish home furnishings but also for its commitment to sustainability. This case study explores IKEA's innovative approach to sustainable interview locations, demonstrating how the company integrates environmental responsibility into its recruitment process.

Green Interviewing Practices:

1. **Sustainable Interview Locations:** IKEA conducts interviews inside certain eco-friendly shops, so exemplifying its dedication to sustainability. These areas are not only conveniently accessible via public transit but also conform to environmentally sustainable construction practices.

2. **Sustainable Materials:** During the interview process, the organization provides applicants with educational materials that are produced using recycled and sustainable resources, so highlighting its commitment to environmentally conscious practices.

3. *Results:* The use of sustainable interviewing procedures by IKEA has not only resulted in a reduction of its environmental effect, but has also garnered positive reception from applicants who align with its sustainability ideals. As a result of this connection, the staff has become more actively involved in IKEA's environmental activities.

Summery

The current chapter has provided an exposition of the pragmatic application of Green HRM concepts within the context of the recruiting and selection procedure. Firms may align their sustainability objectives by choosing applicants that prioritize environmental consciousness and conducting interviews that emphasize eco-friendly practices. This approach enables firms to cultivate a workforce that is in harmony with their sustainability goals. The efficacy of these approaches has been shown via real-world case studies, highlighting that the implementation of green recruiting and selection procedures not only aligns with environmental ideals but also enhances corporate performance and reputation. In the following chapters, we will delve into other dimensions of Green HRM and its profound influence on both businesses and people.

CHAPTER 5: SUSTAINABLE EMPLOYEE ENGAGEMENT

Sustainable employee engagement is an essential component in the formula for achieving corporate success. Employees that are actively involved and committed to their job not only demonstrate higher levels of productivity but also play a significant role in fostering a favorable organizational culture and improving overall performance. Green HRM goes beyond traditional HR practices by including environmental sustainability into employee engagement tactics. By fostering an awareness of environmental responsibility, companies have the potential to instill a profound sense of mission among their personnel, therefore directing their efforts towards the attainment of sustainability objectives.

The Role of Green Employee Engagement Initiatives

1. Wellness Programs with a Green Twist

The integration of environmentally sensitive aspects into wellness programs may provide a twofold effect. Employees get advantages from enhanced bodily and mental well-being, whilst acquiring a more profound comprehension of sustainability concerns. Engaging in activities such as nature walks, practicing yoga in natural environments, or participating in eco-friendly culinary courses may promote both personal well-being and environmental awareness.

2. Sustainability Training and Education

Green HRM include the implementation of training and educational initiatives aimed at empowering employees to make sustainable choices, both inside and outside the confines of the workplace. These programs may include a range of subjects, including waste minimization, energy efficiency, responsible purchasing practices, and the promotion of environmental responsibility. Education plays a crucial role in fostering increased employee engagement in sustainability initiatives.\

3. Environmentally Focused Team-Building Activities

Team-building activities centered on sustainability concerns foster a collaborative environment, stimulate new thinking, and promote collective efforts towards shared objectives among employees. For instance, engaging in activities such as coordinating beach clean-ups, arranging tree planting events, or hosting sustainability-themed hackathons may foster a sense of camaraderie among participants, while simultaneously promoting and furthering sustainability goals.

Case Study 1: Google's Sustainable Wellness Initiatives

Organizational Context: Google, a multinational technology company known for its sustainability efforts.

Green Employee Engagement Initiatives:

1. **Eco-Conscious Wellness Programs:** Google provides a variety of wellness initiatives that include environmentally conscious components. These include outdoor exercise courses held in natural environments, guided mindfulness sessions conducted in green places, and sustainable culinary seminars that prioritize both health and eco-friendly dietary choices.

2. **Sustainability Training:** The organization offers its staff the opportunity to engage in complete sustainability training courses. The aforementioned concerns include a broad

spectrum, including but not limited to energy saving, trash reduction, and sustainable commute alternatives.

Results: The sustainable wellness efforts implemented by Google have resulted in enhanced staff well-being and an increased awareness of environmental stewardship. There is evidence to suggest that employees have elevated levels of job satisfaction and heightened engagement when they are involved in sustainability projects, both inside and outside the confines of their organization.

Case Study 2: Patagonia's Sustainability-Focused Team Building

Organizational Context: Patagonia, an outdoor clothing and gear company known for its strong environmental commitment.

Green Team-Building Initiatives:

1. **Environmental Challenges:** Patagonia arranges environmental initiatives for company employees, including outdoor trips focused on the principle of "Leave No Trace" and "Fix-It Clinics" aimed at repairing and repurposing outdoor equipment.

2. **Sustainability Hackathons:** The organization organizes hackathons with a sustainability emphasis, whereby interdisciplinary teams collaborate to devise inventive resolutions for sustainability-related issues.

Results: The implementation of sustainability-focused team-building activities at Patagonia has resulted in the enhancement of collaboration, the promotion of innovative problem-solving approaches, and the cultivation of a stronger sense of commitment among employees towards the company's environmental objective. These initiatives have a long-term influence, fostering a sense of inspiration among employees to adopt more sustainable lifestyles outside their professional sphere.

Nurturing a Culture of Sustainability

The cultivation of sustainable employee involvement extends beyond the implementation of isolated projects, including the development of a sustainable culture inside the organizational framework.

1. Leadership Commitment

The importance of leadership dedication to sustainability cannot be overstated. When leaders and managers openly exhibit their commitment to environmentally responsible activities, it serves as a source of inspiration for employees, encouraging them to adopt similar behaviors.

2. Open Communication and Recognition

Organizations that successfully communicate their sustainability successes and acknowledge the efforts of their employees are able to cultivate a culture that prioritizes sustainability. This fosters a persistent commitment and endeavors towards achieving sustainable objectives.

3. Employee Involvement and Input

The inclusion of employees in the development of sustainability policies and activities fosters a feeling of ownership and pride among them, as they see their efforts as valuable to the organization's environmental objectives.

Summery

This chapter has examined the significant role of Green HRM in promoting sustainable employee engagement. Organizations enable their employees to become champions for good change by integrating eco-friendly components into wellness programs, offering sustainability training, and facilitating team-building events with an environmental emphasis. These activities not only contribute to the improvement of well-being and work happiness, but also foster a stronger dedication among employees towards achieving sustainable objectives. In addition, through the cultivation of a sustainable culture, guided by dedicated leadership, open communication, and active employee participation, organizations have the potential to foster a workforce that is not only actively involved but also deeply enthusiastic about promoting environmental stewardship, both within the organization and in the broader community. In the next chapters, we will further examine the many effects of Green HRM on firms, employees, and the wider society.

CHAPTER 6: GREEN TRAINING AND DEVELOPMENT

In the current epoch characterized by a heightened emphasis on environmental sustainability, it is essential for enterprises to guarantee that their personnel have the requisite knowledge and competencies to effectively spearhead sustainability endeavors. The concept of Green HRM encompasses the integration of eco-conscious practices into the realm of training and development, hence fostering the creation of a learning environment that is more sustainable in nature.

Designing Eco-Friendly Training Programs

1. Sustainable Learning Materials

The use of digital learning materials not only mitigates the environmental impact associated with paper waste but also enhances accessibility and permits seamless updating. E-books, online modules, and interactive digital information serve as environmentally sustainable alternatives to conventional printed materials.

2. Virtual Training

Virtual training solutions are an efficient approach to deliver learning opportunities while lowering environmental impact. Webinars, online courses, and virtual classrooms allow participants to study from the comfort of their own locations, reducing down on travel-related emissions.

3. Sustainability-Focused Content

It is important to ensure that training programs are designed to include sustainability concepts, including many aspects such as energy saving, waste reduction, ethical procurement, and environmental stewardship. This program provides employees with the necessary knowledge to effectively contribute to environmental projects.

Leveraging Technology for Reduced Carbon Footprint

1. E-Learning Platforms

E-learning platforms provide a scalable and ecologically sustainable method for facilitating training and development. The use of digital resources and online platforms leads to a decrease in the need for physical printed materials and transportation, hence contributing to a reduction in carbon emissions.

2. Virtual Reality and Augmented Reality

Organizations has the potential to use Virtual Reality (VR) and Augmented Reality (AR) technology in order to create immersive training simulations that successfully captivate employees in sustainability scenarios, hence boosting experiential learning and fostering environmental awareness.

Sustainability in Leadership Development

1. Leadership Programs with a Sustainability Focus

It is recommended that leadership development programs include modules centered on sustainability, which aim to enhance leaders' comprehension of the environmental issues and possibilities that pertain to their respective professions.

2. Leading by Example

Leaders who exemplify sustainable behaviors and incorporate environmentally conscious ideas into their decision-making processes serve as role models, motivating others to adopt similar practices. This, in turn, strengthens a culture that prioritizes sustainability.

Case Study 1: Microsoft's Sustainable E-Learning Initiatives

Organizational Context: Microsoft, a multinational technology company.

Green Training Initiatives:

1. **Digital Learning Materials:** Microsoft transitioned their training materials from traditional print formats to digital resources, including interactive e-learning modules, webinars, and digital textbooks. The implementation of this shift resulted in a substantial decrease in paper waste.

2. **Virtual Training:** The organization used virtual training programs, facilitating the inclusion of personnel from various geographical locations in training sessions without necessitating travel. As a consequence, there was a decrease in carbon emissions linked to transportation for commute purposes and the choice of location.

Results: The sustainable e-learning efforts implemented by Microsoft resulted in a reduction in the company's environmental footprint, while simultaneously improving the accessibility and efficacy of its training programs. The employees were able to learn more skills and knowledge while simultaneously reducing their carbon impact.

Case Study 2: Interface's Leadership Development for Sustainability

Organizational Context: Interface Inc. is a multinational flooring producer that has emerged as a prominent exemplar of sustainability and environmental responsibility within the business sphere. Central to its transition towards sustainability is the implementation of its Leadership Development program. This case study examines the impact of Interface's Leadership Development programs on the company's dedication to sustainability.

Background of Interface's Sustainability Journey:

The sustainability journey of Interface began during the 1990s, after a transformational commitment made by the company's founder and visionary leader, Ray Anderson, to transition into a "restorative enterprise." The objective of this pledge was to achieve a state of zero adverse environmental effects by the year 2020, sometimes referred to as the "Mission Zero" project.

Sustainability in Leadership Development: In order to further the sustainability mission, Interface has created a comprehensive Leadership Development program aimed at cultivating a culture of sustainability throughout its workforce

1. **Sustainability Modules:** Interface incorporated sustainability-focused modules into its leadership development programs. These modules covered topics such as sustainable supply chain management, circular economy principles, and environmental stewardship.

2. **Leading by Example:** Interface's top leaders actively embraced sustainable practices, setting an example for the entire organization. They made sustainability a central focus of their decision-making processes and communicated its importance to employees.

Results: The Leadership Development program offered by Interface has played a crucial role in influencing the company's progression towards sustainability. Interface has effectively proven that corporate sustainability can transcend being a mere objective, and instead, be deeply ingrained into a company's core values and achievements, achieved via forward-thinking leadership, educational initiatives, practical implementation, and fostering a sustainable culture. This case study presents Interface Inc. as an exemplary illustration of how a dedication to sustainability, when integrated into the development of leadership, may facilitate profound organizational transformation and contribute to a more sustainable future for the globe.

Conclusion

This chapter has provided insight into the significance of Green HRM in the context of training and development endeavors. Organizations may foster a workforce capable of driving sustainable change by implementing eco-friendly training programs, using technology to minimize the carbon footprint associated with learning, and integrating sustainability ideas into leadership development initiatives. These practices not only demonstrate a commitment to environmental ideals but also contribute to the improved accessibility and efficacy of training programs. In addition, leadership development with a focus on sustainability ensures that leaders has the necessary skills and abilities to successfully guide the business in achieving its sustainability objectives. In the subsequent chapters, we will further examine the many ramifications of Green HRM on various stakeholders, including companies, employees, and the wider society.

CHAPTER 7: SUSTAINABLE PERFORMANCE MANAGEMENT

Sustainable Performance Management is a strategy framework that incorporates sustainability ideas into an organization's performance assessment and management procedures. This statement underscores the need for enterprises to not just prioritize their financial success, but also to take into account their environmental and social implications. The aforementioned notion is in accordance with the triple bottom line framework, which encompasses the consideration of economic, environmental, and social elements in the assessment of organizational performance. Sustainable Performance Management encompasses the integration of sustainability measures and indicators into key performance indicators, hence assuring the alignment of sustainability objectives with the overarching strategy of the firm (Epstein & Roy, 2001). Stakeholder involvement plays a pivotal role in businesses as it facilitates the comprehension and resolution of the many expectations held by stakeholders such as employees, consumers, investors, and communities. This method has advantages such as the acquisition of a competitive edge, the reduction of risks, and the improvement of long-term sustainability. In general, Sustainable Performance Management aids companies in achieving a harmonious integration of economic success, environmental stewardship, and social responsibility, hence facilitating the attainment of sustainable development objectives.

Integration of Sustainability Metrics

1. Sustainability Key Performance Indicators (KPIs)

The use of sustainability Key Performance Indicators (KPIs), such as energy conservation, waste minimization, and carbon emissions reduction, inside performance evaluations guarantees that employees' assessments are contingent upon their contributions towards sustainability objectives.

2. Environmental Impact Measurement

The quantification of employees' environmental effects, including factors like as energy use, paper usage, and commuting patterns, offers a concrete means of evaluating their role in promoting sustainability and establishing goals for improvement.

Feedback for Eco-conscious Behaviors

1. Regular Sustainability Feedback

Providing consistent feedback about sustainability-related activities and accomplishments serves to maintain employee involvement in environmentally aware projects and cultivates a climate of ongoing improvement.

2. Recognition and Rewards

The practice of recognizing and offering rewards to workers for their contributions in advancing sustainability initiatives helps to foster environmentally conscious behaviors and acts as a catalyst for inspiring others to follow suit.

Setting Sustainability-Related Goals

1. Personal Sustainability Goals

Enabling employee to set their own sustainability objectives fosters a sense of ownership and dedication towards environmental accountability.

2. Incorporating Sustainability into Development Plans

The integration of sustainability into employee's development plans serves as a testament to the organization's dedication to nurturing environmentally sensitive skills and abilities.

Case Study 1: Unilever's Sustainability Metrics in Performance Management

Organizational Context: Unilever, a renowned multinational firm working in the consumer goods market, has gained extensive global recognition and praise for its steadfast commitment to the ideals of sustainability. This case study examines the integration of sustainability measures into Unilever's performance management system, demonstrating the company's commitment to harmonizing environmental and social responsibility with its commercial practices.

Developing the Agenda for Sustainability:

The trajectory of Unilever's commitment to sustainability can be traced back to the inception of its ambitious Sustainable Living Plan in 2010. The aforementioned strategy delineated explicit objectives pertaining to sustainability, including the reduction of the company's ecological footprint and the enhancement of the societal implications associated with its goods.

Sustainable Performance Management Initiatives:

1. **Sustainability KPIs:** Unilever incorporates key performance indicators (KPIs) related to sustainability inside its performance management framework. Employees are assessed not just on conventional metrics, but also on their involvement in sustainability objectives, including the reduction of water use, waste minimization, and the procurement of sustainable products.

2. **Regular Sustainability Feedback:** Unilever offers its employees monthly feedback about their environmentally mindful practices. This feedback facilitates employees'

comprehension of their influence on sustainability and serves as a source of motivation for them to consistently enhance their efforts.

Results: The implementation of Unilever's sustainable performance management methodology has resulted in notable advancements towards the attainment of its sustainability goals. The employees are actively involved in sustainability projects, demonstrating a strong alignment with the company's dedication to environmental responsibility.

Case Study 2: IBM's Sustainability-Related Goal Setting

Organizational Context: IBM, a multinational corporation specializing in technology and consulting services, has shown a robust dedication to sustainability by implementing a wide range of goal-oriented activities. This case study examines the use of sustainability-related goal setting by IBM to promote environmental and social responsibility, therefore showcasing the company's commitment to becoming a leader in sustainability.

The Journey of IBM Sustainability:

The trajectory of IBM's commitment to sustainability may be traced back to its early acknowledgement of environmental and social obligations. The organization has constantly endeavored to develop creative solutions in order to effectively tackle global concerns. A significant turning point occurred in 1971 when the company introduced its Environmental Affairs program, which placed a strong emphasis on integrating sustainability principles into its corporate culture.

Sustainability-Related Goal Setting:

1. **Personal Sustainability Goals:** IBM promotes a corporate culture that empowers its employees to establish individual objectives pertaining to sustainability. This enables people to assume responsibility for their environmentally responsible acts and links their endeavors with the sustainability purpose of the company.

2. **Incorporating Sustainability into Development Plans:** The integration of sustainability goals is included into the development plans of employees. IBM offers a comprehensive range of tools, training opportunities, and support mechanisms to facilitate the attainment of employees' objectives.

Results: IBM's prioritization of goal formulation pertaining to sustainability has resulted in the development of a workforce that is not only in accordance with the organization's sustainability goals but also equipped with the authority to enact significant environmental transformations. The aforementioned strategy has played a significant role in establishing IBM as a prominent figure in the realm of sustainability.

Summary

This chapter has elucidated the significance of Green HRM in the context of sustainable performance management. Organizations may effectively foster environmentally responsible behaviors among employees by incorporating sustainability indicators, offering consistent feedback on eco-conscious activities, and establishing sustainability-oriented objectives. Empirical evidence from real-world case studies showcases the efficacy of these techniques in facilitating substantial advancements towards sustainable goals. By implementing sustainable performance management, firms are able to improve their environmental footprint while simultaneously cultivating a sustainable culture that is fundamental to their overall achievements. In the subsequent chapters, we will further examine the many ramifications of Green HRM on various stakeholders, including companies, employees, and the wider society.

CHAPTER 8: GREEN COMPENSATION AND BENEFITS

Compensation and benefits have a crucial role in the recruitment, retention, and motivation of employees. Green HRM expands upon these ideas by including pay and benefits systems that incentivize and acknowledge environmentally conscientious behaviour. Organizations may cultivate a culture of environmental responsibility by formulating pay packages that prioritize eco-friendliness and establishing sustainable incentive programs.

Designing Eco-friendly Compensation Packages

1. Pay-for-Sustainability

The implementation of pay-for-sustainability models involves the integration of a fraction of an employee's remuneration with the attainment of sustainability objectives, either at an individual or team level. These objectives include several sustainability goals, including but not limited to the reduction of energy consumption and the fulfillment of waste reduction targets.

2. Environmental Stipends

Providing monetary incentives in the form of stipends to promote environmentally conscious actions, such as using public transportation or enhancing residential energy efficiency, may effectively harmonize remuneration practices with sustainability goals.

Implementing Sustainable Incentive Programs

1. Performance Bonuses for Sustainability

To enhance employee engagement and foster a culture of environmental responsibility, it is recommended to include sustainability-specific performance incentives inside existing incentive programs. This strategic approach aims to incentivize employees to actively participate in and contribute towards achieving environmental objectives.

2. Green Teams and Recognition

Promote the establishment of environmentally-focused teams within the organizational framework and acknowledge their contributions to sustainability endeavors by implementing reward systems or recognition initiatives.

Green Perks for Attraction and Retention

1. Eco-friendly Commuting Support

The provision of sustainable commuting assistance showcases an organization's dedication to environmental sustainability and has the potential to appeal to those who prioritize ecological consciousness.

2. Sustainable Workplace Amenities

The objective is to provide a workplace that integrates sustainable facilities, so creating an appealing atmosphere for employees and aligning with their environmentally aware principles.

Case Study 1: Patagonia's Pay-for-Sustainability Model

Organizational Context: Patagonia is a renowned firm specializing in outdoor clothes and accessories, recognized for its notable dedication to environmental sustainability.

Eco-friendly Compensation Package:

1. **Pay-for-Sustainability:** The "Pay-for-Sustainability" concept used by Patagonia is shown via many initiatives, such as the "1% for the Planet" campaign, whereby the firm allocates 1% of its yearly sales towards supporting environmental issues. Furthermore, Patagonia has adopted the "Worn Wear" project, with the objective of encouraging customers to acquire pre-owned Patagonia products and engage in the exchange of their previously owned things. This model advocates for the adoption of sustainable consumption practices and the mitigation of waste generation.

Results: The implementation of Patagonia's remuneration system based on sustainability has effectively incentivized staff to actively engage in environmental efforts. The correlation between remuneration and sustainability performance has engendered a staff that exhibits a profound dedication to the organization's environmental objective.

Case Study 2: Salesforce's Sustainable Incentive Programs

Organizational Context: Salesforce, a prominent multinational enterprise specializing in the development and provision of customer relationship management (CRM) software, has garnered considerable recognition for its pioneering technological advancements as well as its unwavering dedication to sustainability. This case study investigates the Sustainable Incentive Programs implemented by Salesforce. These programs exemplify the company's commitment to integrating corporate success with environmental and social responsibility, supported by measurable outcomes and beneficial effects.

Sustainable Incentive Programs:

1. **Performance Bonuses for Sustainability:** Salesforce provides performance incentives that are contingent upon the attainment of sustainability accomplishments. Employees are

provided with monetary incentives for achieving or surpassing sustainability objectives, such as the reduction of greenhouse gas emissions.

Results: Salesforce's sustainable incentive programs have effectively contributed to the advancement of sustainability initiatives. The staff is driven to engage actively in the attainment of the organization's environmental goals, hence leading to the establishment of a more sustainable work environment and operational practices.

Summary

This chapter has elucidated the use of Green HRM in the context of compensation and benefits systems, with the aim of fostering environmental responsibility. Organizations may link their pay strategies with sustainability goals by including eco-friendly remuneration packages, developing sustainable incentive programs, and providing green benefits for the sake of attraction and retention. These practices serve as a source of motivation for employees to actively participate in achieving environmental objectives, while also acting as a means to recruit and retain highly skilled individuals who align with the organization's environmentally aware ideals. By implementing this alignment, companies have the ability to cultivate a workforce that is not just actively involved but also profoundly dedicated to promoting and advancing beneficial environmental transformations. In the following chapters, we will further examine the many ramifications of Green HRM on various aspects such as companies, employees, and the wider global context.

CHAPTER 9: GREEN WORKPLACE CULTURE

The term "Green Workplace Culture" encompasses a collection of principles, actions, and attitudes shown by an institution, which put significant emphasis on the preservation of the environment and the fulfillment of ecological obligations. The prevailing culture within this firm fosters a collective commitment among employees to reduce their ecological impact and prioritize environmentally responsible choices across all facets of their professional endeavors. The implementation of a green workplace culture yields advantages not only for environmental sustainability, but also for the overall welfare of employees and the financial performance of the organization. Green HRM plays a crucial role in fostering and advancing this culture throughout a firm.

Leadership's Role in Fostering Environmental Consciousness

1. Leading by Example

Leaders that exhibit a steadfast dedication to sustainability via their behaviors serve as a source of inspiration for staff, motivating them to emulate such practices. This entails the adoption of environmentally friendly practices in both professional and personal domains.

2. Sustainability Champions

The act of designating employees as sustainability champions entails formally assigning them a role in advocating for and advancing green principles and practices. These people have the capacity to serve as role models and proactively involve their colleagues in endeavors related to sustainability.

Importance of Communication in Building a Culture of Sustainability

1. Transparent Communication

Open and clear communication on sustainability projects cultivates a feeling of inclusivity and collective purpose among staff. The provision of information and engagement in the organization's environmental initiatives are facilitated via this mechanism.

2. Employee Input and Feedback

The integration of employee participation in the process of sustainability planning and decision-making fosters a sense of value and commitment among employees towards the organization's environmental objectives.

Integration of Green Values into Mission and Vision

1. Mission Statement

The inclusion of environmental sustainability in a mission statement serves to emphasize its significance and establish a congruence between the company and environmentally conscious principles.

2. Vision for Sustainability

A vision for sustainability functions as a guiding principle, offering employees a comprehensive comprehension of the organization's dedication to environmentally sensitive operations and enduring environmental goals.

Case Study 1: Patagonia's Leadership in Environmental Consciousness

Organizational Context: Patagonia, an outdoor clothing and gear company renowned for its strong environmental commitment.

Leadership's Role:

1. **Leading by Example:** Yvon Chouinard, the creator of Patagonia, has emerged as a prominent proponent of environmental stewardship, actively promoting and personally adopting eco-conscious methods. This commitment establishes the overall ethos of the whole business.

2. **Sustainability Champions:** Patagonia grants its staff the authority to assume the role of environmental advocates. These professionals proactively include their colleagues in environmental activities, cultivating a culture of sustainability internally.

Case Study 2: Interface's Integrated Mission for Sustainability

Organizational Context: Interface, a global flooring company known for its sustainability efforts.

Integration of Green Values:

1. **Mission Statement:** The mission statement of Interface incorporates a steadfast dedication to the principles of sustainability. The statement underscores the organization's commitment to mitigating its adverse ecological effects and fostering a beneficial influence.

2. **Vision for Sustainability:** Interface's commitment to sustainability is shown by their "Mission Zero" initiative, which strives to attain a state of zero environmental impact by the year 2020. The company's sustainability activities are guided by this lofty ambition.

Summary

This chapter has examined the establishment of an environmentally conscious workplace culture via the implementation of Green HRM. Organizations may build a culture of sustainability by placing emphasis on the role of leadership in encouraging environmental awareness, supporting honest communication, and incorporating green principles into the organization's goal and vision. Case studies have provided evidence of organizations that effectively exemplify these concepts, so illustrating the profound impact of a sustainable workplace culture. In the subsequent chapters, we will further examine the many ramifications of Green HRM on various stakeholders, including companies, employees, and the wider global community.

CHAPTER 10: OVERCOMING CHALLENGES AND FUTURE TRENDS

This last chapter focuses on the obstacles and emerging patterns within the field of Green HRM. This study investigates the possible challenges that businesses may face throughout their pursuit of sustainability, including factors such as resistance to change and the intricacies associated with quantifying environmental effect. Furthermore, we provide significant perspectives on the dynamic nature of Green HRM, including the incorporation of state-of-the-art technologies like artificial intelligence, blockchain, and big data analytics to propel sustainability objectives. This chapter provides a pragmatic guide for firms aiming to overcome obstacles and maintain a leading position in environmentally aware human resources operations.

Challenges and Future Trends of Green HRM

1. Challenges in Green HRM:

- **Resistance to Change:** Frequently, the primary challenge lies in the inherent inclination of individuals to exhibit resistance towards change. Employees may exhibit reluctance in embracing novel environmentally-friendly activities as a result of inadequate comprehension, preference for established routines, or apprehensions around prospective increases in effort.

- **Complexities in Measuring Environmental Impact:** The task of quantifying the precise environmental implications of human resource policies may pose significant difficulties. The absence of universally accepted measurement standards and the potential limitations of multiple measures may hinder the comprehensive assessment of an organization's environmental impact.

- **Financial Impediments:** The implementation of green HRM practices may need an initial financial investment. While many firms may be deterred by the initial cost, it is important to note that there might be long-term savings.

- **Lack of Awareness and Training:** Numerous firms may possess little awareness of green HRM or encounter constraints in terms of resources and expertise required for the implementation of such practices.

- **Cultural Barriers:** Cultural disparities within some firms, particularly those with global operations, may impede the implementation of standardized green HRM standards.

2. Future Trends in Green HRM:

- **Artificial Intelligence (AI) in Green HRM:** Artificial intelligence (AI) has the potential to automate and optimize many processes, leading to a reduction in resource usage. According to Smith et al. (2020), the use of predictive analytics enables the anticipation of energy requirements, whilst the implementation of artificial intelligence (AI)-driven bots facilitates the dissemination of knowledge about sustainable practices among personnel.

- **Blockchain for Transparency and Accountability:** The use of blockchain technology inside the supply chain may effectively establish a state of transparency, therefore ensuring that all entities involved in the chain are in compliance with sustainable standards. Additionally, it has the potential to allow stakeholders to authenticate an organization's environmental sustainability credentials.

- **Big Data Analytics:** Through the use of big data, firms have the potential to get valuable information pertaining to several aspects such as their carbon footprints, energy usage, and waste creation. The use of data-driven insights may facilitate the process of making well-informed choices pertaining to sustainability.

- **Employee Engagement Platforms:** Digital platforms and applications have the potential to be designed and implemented in order to actively include employees in sustainability programs, monitor and assess their individual contributions, and provide incentives for adopting eco-friendly behavior.

Summary

Although there exist some obstacles in the adoption and implementation of Green HRM, the outlook for the future is optimistic due to the influential role of technology improvements in driving transformative processes. In order to maintain a competitive edge, organizations must not only possess knowledge of these difficulties, but also actively pursue new solutions, capitalizing on growing trends within the industry.

Corporate Example of Green HRM practices

Example 1: Infosys, a multinational IT services and consulting company

A number of Indian enterprises have adopted Green HRM practices as a means to showcase their commitment towards sustainability and environmental responsibility. An exemplar case may be seen in the form of Infosys, a multinational enterprise that specializes in the provision of information technology services and consulting. The company's central administrative center is situated in Bengaluru, India. Infosys is well recognized for its comprehensive adoption of Green HRM initiatives. The aforementioned organization employs many practices, which are outlined below:

1. **Green Recruitment and Training:** Infosys integrates sustainability ideas inside their recruiting process. The organization recruits people who have a shared dedication to environmental responsibility. Additionally, the organization offers training and development initiatives aimed at augmenting workers' understanding of sustainable practices and the significance of environmental preservation.

2. **Eco-Friendly Workplace:** Infosys has made investments in the establishment of environmentally sustainable work environments. The campuses are intentionally constructed to prioritize sustainability, including elements such as environmentally-friendly structures, energy-efficient lighting systems, and water conservation strategies. The organization advocates for the adoption of environmentally-friendly commuting alternatives among its staff, including the implementation of carpooling initiatives and the use of electric cars on company premises.

3. **Sustainable Employee Engagement:** Infosys promotes and fosters employee engagement in sustainability endeavors. The organization arranges various events,

seminars, and awareness campaigns with the aim of involving workers in activities related to environmental protection. The organization promotes employee engagement in activities such as tree-planting campaigns, trash reduction efforts, and many other environmentally conscious endeavors.

4. **Green Policies and Reporting:** The organization has clearly established rules pertaining to environmental sustainability, including waste minimization, energy conservation, and ethical procurement practices. Additionally, they consistently provide updates on their environmental performance and advancements in achieving sustainability objectives.

5. **Green Data Centers:** Infosys has constructed energy-efficient data centers that use renewable energy sources and modern cooling technology in order to mitigate their environmental impact by minimizing carbon emissions. The architecture of these data centers is aimed at reducing energy usage and mitigating environmental effect.

6. **Supplier Sustainability:** Infosys engages in the assessment and partnership with suppliers and providers that have a shared commitment to sustainability. Suppliers are encouraged to embrace ecologically friendly practices and mitigate their carbon emissions.

7. **Employee Incentives:** Infosys provides incentives and prizes to workers who actively contribute to sustainability initiatives inside the organization. The acknowledgment and valuation of employees' contributions to green projects play a pivotal role in creating a corporate climate that prioritizes and promotes environmental responsibility.

Infosys exemplifies an Indian corporation that has adopted Green HRM practices. Numerous companies in India, notably those operating in the IT industry, have also embraced comparable endeavors aimed at mitigating their ecological footprint and fostering sustainability inside their work environments. These practices are in accordance with India's overarching sustainability objectives and contribute to a corporate climate that is more ecologically conscious.

Example 2: ITC Limited

ITC Limited, a diverse conglomerate operating in several areas such as agriculture, consumer products, and hotels, stands out as a prominent Indian corporate entity that has adopted Green Human Resource Management (Green HRM) techniques. ITC is renowned for its steadfast dedication to sustainability and environmental stewardship, shown by the incorporation of Green HRM practices into its operational framework. The following are the fundamental components of ITC's Green Human Resource Management (HRM) initiatives:

1. **Sustainable Recruitment:** The recruitment process at ITC is characterized by a significant focus on attracting employees who demonstrate alignment with the organization's sustainability objectives. The organization seeks individuals who demonstrate a shared dedication to environmental and social responsibility, aligning with ITC's values.

2. **Employee Training and Development:** The International Trade Commission (ITC) allocates resources towards the implementation of training and development initiatives that prioritize the areas of sustainability and environmental management. The employees are provided with education on environmentally sustainable practices and are actively encouraged to integrate these practices into their work.

3. **Green Workspaces:** ITC has implemented measures aimed at establishing environmentally friendly and sustainable workplace environments. The office buildings are purposefully intended to optimize energy consumption and promote environmental sustainability. Notable characteristics include the strategic use of natural lighting,

implementation of efficient HVAC systems, and incorporation of eco-friendly landscaping.

4. **Employee Engagement:** ITC actively involves its workers in a range of environmentally conscious endeavors, including efforts such as tree-planting campaigns, trash reduction programs, and community engagement projects that prioritize the preservation of the environment. This cultivates a perception of accountability and involvement within the workforce.

5. **Sustainability Reporting:** The Corporation produces yearly sustainability reports that provide comprehensive information on its environmental and social performance. The reports provide a comprehensive range of data pertaining to energy usage, emissions reduction, water conservation, and several other sustainability measures.

6. **Supplier Sustainability:** The International Trade Commission (ITC) engages in collaborative partnerships with suppliers and vendors who demonstrate a commitment to sustainable and environmentally responsible practices. Their primary purpose is to verify that the supply chain is in accordance with ITC's sustainability objectives.

7. **Carbon Neutrality Commitment:** The International Trade Commission (ITC) has made a firm commitment to achieving carbon neutrality throughout its operations. In order to accomplish this objective, the organization is actively engaged in the reduction of their carbon emissions and allocating resources towards the development of renewable energy initiatives.

8. **Corporate Social Responsibility (CSR):** CSR projects undertaken by ITC often exhibit a notable emphasis on environmental concerns. The organization provides assistance for

initiatives pertaining to afforestation, watershed management, and sustainable agriculture, so making a significant contribution towards enhancing the overall sustainability of the communities in which they are involved.

The Green HRM practices implemented by ITC exemplify the company's commitment to sustainability and environmental care. By integrating these practices into its human resources policies and operations, ITC not only fosters a sustainable work culture but also establishes a precedent for other Indian firms to emulate in their endeavor to uphold environmental responsibility.

Example 3: Tata Group

The Tata Group, a diverse conglomerate operating in many industries such as steel, automotive, information technology, and hospitality, serves as a notable illustration of Green HRM methods in India. The Tata Group has a notable and extensive track record of engaging in corporate social responsibility and sustainability initiatives. As part of its operational framework, the organization has successfully incorporated Green HRM principles. The following are many significant components of Tata Group's Green Human Resource Management (HRM) initiatives:

1. **Sustainable Recruitment:** The Tata Group puts significant importance on the recruitment of personnel who demonstrate alignment with the company's sustainability objectives. The organization seeks individuals who demonstrate a shared dedication to Tata's principles of environmental and social accountability.

2. **Employee Training and Development:** The Tata Group allocates resources towards the implementation of training and development initiatives that prioritize the areas of sustainability and environmental management. The workforce is provided with education on environmentally sustainable practices and actively encouraged to integrate them into their professional activities.

3. **Green Workspaces:** The Tata Group has implemented measures aimed at establishing environmentally friendly and sustainable workplace environments. The office buildings are specifically intended to optimize energy consumption and promote environmental sustainability. These structures integrate several elements, such as the use of natural light, the implementation of efficient HVAC systems, and the incorporation of eco-friendly landscaping.

4. **Employee Engagement:** The Tata Group actively involves its workers in a range of environmentally conscious endeavors, including efforts such as tree-planting campaigns, waste minimization programs, and community outreach endeavors centered on the preservation of the environment. This practice cultivates a perception of accountability and active involvement within the workforce.

5. **Sustainability Reporting:** The organization produces yearly sustainability reports that provide comprehensive information on its environmental and social performance. The reports provide a comprehensive range of information pertaining to energy use, emissions reduction, water conservation, and several other sustainability measures.

6. **Supplier and Vendor Sustainability:** The Tata Group engages in collaborations with suppliers and partners that demonstrate a commitment to sustainable and environmentally conscious practices. Their primary mission is to guarantee that the supply chain is in accordance with Tata's sustainability goals.

7. **Carbon Neutrality Commitment:** The Tata Group has made explicit pledges to mitigate its carbon emissions and allocate resources towards the development and use of renewable energy sources. Their objective is to attain carbon neutrality in their operational activities.

8. **Community Development:** The sustainability activities of Tata Group include the communities in which they are situated. The organization provides assistance to a range of initiatives pertaining to environmental preservation, educational advancement, healthcare provision, and social welfare, therefore making a substantial contribution to the holistic welfare of society.

9. **Employee Wellness:** The Tata Group actively supports the well-being of its employees, including both their physical and emotional health. These projects often include environmentally friendly and sustainable components, such as wellness programs that promote physical exercise and stress reduction in natural environments.

The Tata Group is an enterprise that is committed to sustainability, environmental stewardship, and social responsibility, and the Green HRM practices that they apply are an example of this dedication. Through the integration of these practices into its human resources policies and operations, Tata Group not only fosters a sustainable work culture but also establishes a precedent for other Indian firms to emulate in their endeavor to uphold environmental accountability.

Example 4: Wipro Limited, a multinational IT services and consulting company

Wipro Limited, a global IT services and consulting business based in Bengaluru, India, is among the Indian firms that have adopted Green Human Resource Management (Green HRM) techniques. Wipro has garnered recognition for its steadfast dedication to sustainability and its conscientious approach towards environmental responsibility. The following are many significant components of Wipro's Green Human Resource Management (HRM) initiatives:

1. **Sustainable Recruitment:** Wipro places emphasis on the recruitment of employees who demonstrate a shared commitment to the principles of sustainability and environmental stewardship. The organization is in search of individuals who demonstrate alignment with Wipro's environmentally conscious principles.

2. **Employee Training and Development:** Wipro allocates resources towards the implementation of training and development initiatives that prioritize the principles of sustainability and environmental management. The workforce is provided with education on environmentally sustainable practices and actively motivated to integrate them into their professional responsibilities.

3. **Green Workspaces:** The organization has implemented measures to establish environmentally sustainable workplace environments. The campuses have been intentionally developed with a focus on energy efficiency and environmental sustainability. Notable elements include the integration of green buildings, use of natural lighting, and implementation of energy-saving technology.

4. **Employee Engagement:** Wipro actively involves its workers in a range of environmentally conscious endeavors, including efforts like as tree-planting campaigns, waste minimization programs, and community engagement endeavors centered on the preservation of the environment. This cultivates a perception of accountability and involvement within the workforce.

5. **Sustainability Reporting:** Wipro releases yearly sustainability reports that provide comprehensive information on company environmental and social performance. The reports provide a comprehensive range of information pertaining to energy use, emissions reduction, water conservation, and several other sustainability measures.

6. **Supplier and Vendor Sustainability:** Wipro engages in partnerships with suppliers and vendors that adhere to sustainable and environmentally conscious practices. Their efforts are focused on ensuring that the supply chain is in accordance with Wipro's sustainability goals.

7. **Carbon Neutrality Commitment:** Wipro has made a firm commitment to attaining carbon neutrality within its operational activities. The organization is now engaged in proactive efforts to mitigate greenhouse gas emissions, while simultaneously allocating resources towards the development of renewable energy initiatives in order to counterbalance their overall carbon impact.

8. **Employee Involvement in Sustainability:** Wipro effectively involves its workers in sustainability endeavors via the establishment of green teams, sustainability committees, and volunteer engagements. This fosters a corporate climate that promotes and cultivates a sense of ecological responsibility among its employees.

9. **Employee Wellness:** Wipro prioritizes the enhancement of employee well-being, including both physical and mental health aspects. Frequently, these projects include environmentally conscious components, such as wellness programs that promote physical exercise within natural environments.

10. **Global Sustainability Initiatives:** Wipro has expanded its sustainability initiatives on a worldwide scale, ensuring that its activities in different countries are in accordance with local environmental rules and objectives pertaining to sustainability.

Wipro's use of Green HRM practices demonstrates a firm commitment to sustainability, environmental stewardship, and corporate social responsibility. By integrating these practices into its human resources policies and operations, Wipro not only fosters a sustainable work culture but also serves as a model for other Indian firms to emulate in their endeavor to uphold environmental responsibility.

Example 5: Mahindra & Mahindra (M&M), a multinational automobile manufacturing corporation

Mahindra & Mahindra (M&M), a global vehicle manufacturing firm based in Mumbai, India, is recognized for its use of Green HRM techniques. M&M has shown its dedication to sustainability and environmental stewardship via a range of Green HRM projects. The following are the fundamental elements of Mahindra & Mahindra's Green HRM practices:

1. **Sustainable Recruitment:** M&M places emphasis on the recruitment of personnel who demonstrate a strong alignment with the company's dedication to sustainability and environmental stewardship. The organization is in search of individuals that align with M&M's principles pertaining to environmentally friendly and sustainable initiatives.

2. **Employee Training and Development:** M&M strategically allocates resources towards training and development initiatives that prioritize sustainability and environmental management. The organization ensures that its employees are well-informed on environmentally sustainable practices and actively promotes their integration within their respective job responsibilities.

3. **Green Workspaces:** The organization has implemented measures to establish workplace premises that are ecologically friendly. The buildings of the organization integrate energy-efficient architectural designs, use renewable energy sources, and implement waste reduction strategies in order to mitigate their environmental footprint.

4. **Employee Engagement:** M&M effectively involves its workers in several environmentally-friendly endeavors, including efforts such as tree-planting campaigns,

trash reduction programs, and community engagement projects centered on the preservation of the environment. This cultivates a perception of ecological accountability among the workforce.

5. **Sustainability Reporting:** M&M regularly releases sustainability reports that provide comprehensive information on its environmental and social performance. The reports provide a comprehensive range of information pertaining to energy use, emissions reduction, water conservation, and several other sustainability measures.

6. **Supplier and Vendor Sustainability:** M&M engages in collaborative partnerships with suppliers and vendors that adhere to sustainable and environmentally conscious methods. In order to connect the supply chain with M&M's sustainability goals, collaborative efforts are undertaken by many stakeholders.

7. **Carbon Neutrality Commitment:** M&M has undertaken initiatives to mitigate its carbon emissions and allocate resources towards the development and use of renewable energy sources. Their objective is to attain carbon neutrality in their operational activities.

8. **Employee Involvement in Sustainability:** M&M fosters a culture of employee engagement in sustainability endeavors by aggressively promoting their involvement in green teams, sustainability committees, and volunteer activities. This fosters a corporate culture that encourages and prioritizes environmental stewardship throughout the workforce.

9. **Community Development:** M&M's sustainability endeavors include the local areas in which they conduct their operations. The organization provides assistance to a range of initiatives pertaining to environmental preservation, educational advancement, healthcare

provision, and social welfare, therefore making a significant contribution to the holistic welfare of the community.

10. **Product Sustainability:** M&M has prioritized the development of sustainable and environmentally-friendly automotive goods, such as electric cars and vehicles with reduced emissions, as an integral component of its comprehensive sustainability initiatives.

The Green HRM practices used by Mahindra & Mahindra demonstrate the company's firm commitment to sustainability, environmental stewardship, and corporate social responsibility. Through the integration of these practices into its human resources policies and operations, M&M effectively fosters a sustainable work culture, therefore serving as a role model for other Indian firms in their endeavor to embrace environmental responsibility.

Example 6: Indian Railways

The Indian Railways serves as a prominent illustration of Green HRM methods inside India. The Indian Railways is globally recognized as one of the biggest and most ancient railway networks, and it has made notable efforts to integrate environmental sustainability into its HRM procedures. The following are significant components of the Green HRM initiatives implemented by Indian Railways:

1. **Training and Awareness:** Indian Railways offers comprehensive training and awareness initiatives to its staff with the aim of promoting environmental conservation and fostering sustainable practices. These programs aim to provide education to workers on eco-friendly efforts and promote the adoption of sustainable practices within their professional activities.

2. **Energy Efficiency:** The Indian Railways has successfully adopted a range of energy-efficient measures in its operational practices, including the adoption of LED lighting, use of energy-efficient locomotives, and the implementation of enhanced energy management systems. HRM procedures include the provision of training to workers on energy-saving strategies, as well as the promotion of energy conservation efforts.

3. **Waste Management:** The railway system has implemented garbage segregation and recycling protocols. HRM is responsible for the education and engagement of workers in waste reduction and correct disposal procedures.

4. **Green Procurement:** Indian Railways promotes the adoption of environmentally friendly and sustainable procurement processes via the acquisition of eco-conscious goods and resources. HRM plays a crucial role in the advocacy and implementation of

sustainable procurement policies inside an organization, aiming to foster environmentally and socially responsible practices among both workers and suppliers.

5. **Biodiversity Conservation:** The operations of Indian Railways often take place within a wide range of ecological settings. Human resource management (HRM) methods include several strategies aimed at raising awareness among personnel about the significance of biodiversity protection and mitigating the adverse effects of railway operations on nearby ecosystems.

6. **Carbon Emission Reduction:** The railway system has undertaken initiatives aimed at mitigating carbon emissions via the use of electric and solar-powered trains. Human resource management (HRM) may include the implementation of training programs aimed at supporting these objectives and mitigating the environmental impact of railway operations.

7. **Employee Engagement:** Indian Railways proactively involves its workforce in environmentally sustainable endeavors. Human Resource Management (HRM) facilitates and encourages employee engagement in various environmental initiatives such as tree-planting efforts, cleaning campaigns, and other related projects.

8. **Sustainability Reporting:** Indian Railways releases sustainability reports in order to monitor and disclose its ecological performance. Human resource management (HRM) might potentially fulfill the function of collecting data and compiling these reports.

9. **Public Awareness:** The human resource management methods used by Indian Railways include initiatives aimed at enhancing passenger and public knowledge of environmental concerns, as well as the railway's steadfast dedication to sustainability.

The Green HRM practices used by Indian Railways exemplify the organization's commitment to environmental sustainability and its efforts to mitigate the ecological consequences associated with one of India's most extensive transportation networks. These practices are in accordance with India's overarching sustainability objectives and serve as a model for other entities within the nation.

REFERENCES

Aguinis, H., & Glavas, A. (2012). What we know and don't know about corporate social responsibility: A review and research agenda. *Journal of Management, 38*(4), 932–968. https://doi.org/10.1177/0149206311436079

Alfes, K., Shantz, A., & Truss, C. (2012). The link between perceived HRM practices, performance and well-being: the moderating effect of trust in the employer: Perceived HRM practices, trust, performance and well-being. *Human Resource Management Journal, 22*(4), 409–427. https://doi.org/10.1111/1748-8583.12005

Amjad, F., Abbas, W., Zia-Ur-Rehman, M., Baig, S. A., Hashim, M., Khan, A., & Rehman, H.-U.-. (2021). Effect of green human resource management practices on organizational sustainability: the mediating role of environmental and employee performance. *Environmental Science and Pollution Research International, 28*(22), 28191–28206. https://doi.org/10.1007/s11356-020-11307-9

Anderson, R. C. (1998). *Mid-course correction: toward a sustainable enterprise: the interface model.*

Archie, B., & Carroll, B. (2014). *Business & society: ethics, sustainability, and stakeholder management.*

Bahuguna, P. C., Srivastava, R., & Tiwari, S. (2023). Two-decade journey of green human resource management research: a bibliometric analysis. *Benchmarking An International Journal, 30*(2), 585–602. https://doi.org/10.1108/bij-10-2021-0619

Banerjee, S., & Chakraborty, D. (2020). Role of Eco-efficiency in evaluating environmental performance and in accomplishing sustainable development goals case study of ITC ltd. *The Management Accountant Journal, 55*(12), 95. https://doi.org/10.33516/maj.v55i12.95-101p

Bansal, P., & Roth, K. (2000). Why companies go green: A model of ecological responsiveness. *Academy of Management Journal, 43*(4), 717–736. https://doi.org/10.2307/1556363

Bauer, T. N., & Erdogan, B. (Eds.). (2015). *The Oxford handbook of leader-member exchange.* Oxford university press.

Becker, B., & Gerhart, B. (1996). The impact of human resource management on organizational performance: Progress and prospects. *Academy of Management Journal, 39*(4), 779–801. https://doi.org/10.2307/256712

Bogart, D., & Chaudhary, L. (2012). Regulation, ownership, and costs: A historical perspective from Indian railways. *American Economic Journal. Economic Policy, 4*(1), 28–57. https://doi.org/10.1257/pol.4.1.28

Budhwar, P. S. (2000). Determinants of HRM policies and practices in India: An empirical study. *Global Business Review, 1*(2), 229–247. https://doi.org/10.1177/097215090000100205

Chaudhary, R. (2019). Green human resource management in Indian automobile industry. *Journal of Global Responsibility, 10*(2), 161–175. https://doi.org/10.1108/jgr-12-2018-0084

Chen, F. H. (2021). Sustainable education through e-learning: The case study of ilearn2. 0. *Sustainability, 13*.

Chouinard, Y. (2016). Let my people go surfing: The education of a reluctant businessman-- including 10 more years of business unusual. *Penguin.*

Cohune, L. (2019). *Stepping Lightly: A Case Study on Patagonia's Corporate Environmental and Social Responsibility Marketing Strategy.*

Daily, B. F., & Huang, S.-C. (2001). Achieving sustainability through attention to human resource factors in environmental management. *International Journal of Operations & Production Management, 21*(12), 1539–1552. https://doi.org/10.1108/01443570110410892

Das, S. C., & Singh, R. (2020). Psychometric testing of the green human resource management (ghrm) scale using indian sample. *JIMS 8M, 25*(3), 4. https://doi.org/10.5958/0973-9343.2020.00018.6

Davenport, T. H. (2018). *The AI advantage: How to put the artificial intelligence revolution to work.* mit Press.

Davenport, Thomas H., Harris, J., & Shapiro, J. (2010). Competing on talent analytics. *Harvard Business Review, 88*(10), 52–58, 150.

Delmas, M. A., & Montes-Sancho, M. J. (2011). US state policies for renewable energy: Context and effectiveness. *Energy Policy, 39*(5), 2273–2288.

Deloitte. (2020). "Is there a future for HR Tech?"

Epstein, M. J., & Roy, M.-J. (2001). Sustainability in action: Identifying and measuring the key performance drivers. *Long Range Planning, 34*(5), 585–604. https://doi.org/10.1016/s0024-6301(01)00084-x

Ergene, S., Banerjee, S. B., & Hoffman, A. J. (2021). Un) sustainability and organization studies: Towards a radical engagement. *Organization Studies, 42*(8), 1319–1335.

Felstead, A., & Henseke, G. (2017). Assessing the growth of remote working and its consequences for effort, well-being and work-life balance. *New Technology, Work and Employment, 32*(3), 195–212. https://doi.org/10.1111/ntwe.12097

Fletcher, L., Alfes, K., & Robinson, D. (2018). The relationship between perceived training and development and employee retention: the mediating role of work attitudes. *The International Journal of Human Resource Management, 29*(18), 2701–2728. https://doi.org/10.1080/09585192.2016.1262888

Fowler, S. J. (2007). Incorporating sustainable business practices into company strategy. *Strategic Direction, 23*(7). https://doi.org/10.1108/sd.2007.05623gad.008

Gadenne, D., Sharma, B., Kerr, D., & Smith, T. (2011). The influence of consumers' environmental beliefs and attitudes on energy saving behaviours. *Energy Policy, 39*(12), 7684–7694. https://doi.org/10.1016/j.enpol.2011.09.002

George, S. (2014). Google Inc.: Not just a search engine, but an engine of strategic product diversification and excellence in corporate strategy. *International Journal of Advanced Research in Management and Social Sciences, 3*(2), 62–81.

Glavas, A. (2012). Employee engagement and sustainability: A model for implementing meaningfulness at and in work. *Journal of Corporate Citizenship, 2012*(46), 13–29. https://doi.org/10.9774/gleaf.4700.2012.su.00003

Hrelja, R., Isaksson, K., & Richardson, T. (2012). IKEA and small city development in Sweden: Planning myths, realities, and unsustainable mobilities. *International Planning Studies, 17*(2), 125–145. https://doi.org/10.1080/13563475.2012.672797

IBM. (2020). IBM Environmental Report

ITC Sustainability Reports. (n.d.). *ITC Sustainability Reports*.

Jabbour, C. J. C. (2013). Environmental training in organisations: From a literature review to a framework for future research. *Resources, Conservation, and Recycling, 74*, 144–155. https://doi.org/10.1016/j.resconrec.2012.12.017

Jabbour, C. J. C., & Santos, F. C. A. (2008). Relationships between human resource dimensions and environmental management in companies: proposal of a model. *Journal of Cleaner Production, 16*(1), 51–58. https://doi.org/10.1016/j.jclepro.2006.07.025

Jackson, E. S., & Robinson, S. L. (2020). Beyond target setting: Extending HRM's role in sustainability through Green HRM. *Human Resource Management Review, 30*(1).

Jackson, S. E., & Ruderman, M. (1999). *Diversity in work teams: Research paradigms for a changing workplace*. American Psychological Association.

Jackson, Susan E., Renwick, D. W. S., Jabbour, C. J. C., & Muller-Camen, M. (2011). State-of-the-art and future directions for Green human resource management: Introduction to the special issue. *German Journal of Human Resource Management, 25*(2), 99–116. https://doi.org/10.1177/239700221102500203

Jackson, Susan E., Schuler, R. S., & Jiang, K. (2014). An aspirational framework for strategic human resource management. *Academy of Management Annals, 8*(1), 1–56. https://doi.org/10.1080/19416520.2014.872335

Jeljeli, R., Farhi, F., Setoutah, S., & Laghouag, A. (2022). Microsoft teams' acceptance for the e-learning purposes during Covid-19 outbreak: A case study of UAE. *International Journal of Data and Network Science, 6*(3), 629–640.

Jones, P., & Smith, A. (2021). The role of big data in Green HRM. *Journal of Organizational Effectiveness: People and Performance, 8*(2), 154–171.

Kshetri, N. (2022). Blockchain systems and ethical sourcing in the mineral and metal industry: a multiple case study. *International Journal of Logistics Management, 33*(1), 1–27. https://doi.org/10.1108/ijlm-02-2021-0108

Lakshmi, V., & Kennedy, H. (2017). The role of business sustainability in human resource management: A study on Indian manufacturing companies. *The South East Asian Journal of Management, 11*(1). https://doi.org/10.21002/seam.v11i1.7739

Lawrence, J., Rasche, A., & Kenny, K. (2019). Sustainability as opportunity: Unilever's sustainable living plan. In *Managing Sustainable Business* (pp. 435–455). Springer Netherlands.

Lewis, R., Donaldson-Feilder, E., & Tharani, T. (2014). Managing for sustainable employee engagement. *CIPD*.

Madhani, P. M. (2017). Enhancing return on salesforce investment: Reallocating incentives and training resources with intrinsic valuation approach. *Compensation and Benefits Review, 49*(3), 135–152. https://doi.org/10.1177/0886368718790294

Maheshwari, S. K., & Ganesh, M. P. (2006). Ethics in organizations: The case of Tata Steel. *Vikalpa The Journal for Decision Makers, 31*(2), 75–88. https://doi.org/10.1177/0256090920060205

Mahindra & Mahindra Sustainability Reports. (Annual reports available on the Mahindra & Mahindra Sustainability). (n.d.).

Marler, J. H., & Boudreau, J. W. (2017). An evidence-based review of HR Analytics. *The International Journal of Human Resource Management, 28*(1), 3–26. https://doi.org/10.1080/09585192.2016.1244699

Mayank, G. (2014). Impact of Working Capital Management Practices of Automobile Firms on their Profitability: An Example of Mahindra & Mahindra Ltd. *Journal Pacific Business Review International, 6*(8), 1–6.

Mwita, K. M., & Kinemo, S. M. (2018). The role of green recruitment and selection on performance of Processing Industries in Tanzania: A case of Tanzania Tobacco Processors Limited (TTPL). *International Journal of Human Resource Studies, 8*(4), 35. https://doi.org/10.5296/ijhrs.v8i4.13356

Nagendra, A., & Kansal, S. (2015). Reducing carbon footprint through green HRM. *SAMVAD, 8.*

Obaid, T. (2015). The impact of green recruitment, green training and green learning on the firm performance: conceptual paper. *International Journal of Applied Research, 1*(12), 951–953.

Paillé, P., Chen, Y., Boiral, O., & Jin, J. (2014). The impact of human resource management on environmental performance: An employee-level study. *Journal of Business Ethics, 121*(3), 451–466. https://doi.org/10.1007/s10551-013-1732-0

Pereira, V. E., Fontinha, R., Budhwar, P., & Arora, B. (2018). Human resource management and performance at the Indian Railways. *Journal of Organizational Change Management, 31*(1), 47–61. https://doi.org/10.1108/jocm-04-2017-0157

Pereira, V., & Fontinha, R. (2016). An exploration of the role duality experienced by HR professionals as both implementers and recipients of HR practices: Evidence from the Indian railways. *Human Resource Management, 55*(1), 127–142. https://doi.org/10.1002/hrm.21717

Perrini, F., & Tencati, A. (2006). Sustainability and stakeholder management: the need for new corporate performance evaluation and reporting systems. *Business Strategy and the Environment, 15*(5), 296–308. https://doi.org/10.1002/bse.538

Pham, D. D. T., & Paillé, P. (2019). Green recruitment and selection: an insight into green patterns. *International Journal of Manpower, 41*(3), 258–272. https://doi.org/10.1108/ijm-05-2018-0155

Poddar, P. (2021). Integrating sustainability into the Textile Supply Chain-comparing the case of H & M and Patagonia. *Scholarly.*

Ponte, S. (2020). Green capital accumulation: Business and sustainability management in a world of global value chains. *New Political Economy*, *25*(1), 72–84. https://doi.org/10.1080/13563467.2019.1581152

Prasad, A., & Kumar, S. (2013). Poverty Alleviation through Corporate Social Responsibility Policy: An Ethnographic Study of Tata Steel Initiatives in a Jamshedpur Village. *Jharkhand Journal of Development and Management Studies*, *11*(2), 5297–5323.

Rajala, R., Westerlund, M., & Lampikoski, T. (2016). Environmental sustainability in industrial manufacturing: re-examining the greening of Interface's business model. *Journal of Cleaner Production*, *115*, 52–61. https://doi.org/10.1016/j.jclepro.2015.12.057

Rasmussen, T., & Ulrich, D. (2015). Learning from practice: how HR analytics avoids being a management fad. *Organizational Dynamics*, *44*(3), 236–242. https://doi.org/10.1016/j.orgdyn.2015.05.008

Rath, T. S., & Padhi, M. (2023). Role of HR in Driving CSR: An In-depth Study of (Comparison Between) Tata Steel and ITC. *NHRD Network Journal*, *16*(2), 164–171.

Raza, K., Patle, V. K., & Arya, S. (2012). A review on green computing for eco-friendly and sustainable it. *Journal of Computational Intelligence and Electronic Systems*, *1*(1), 3–16.

Renwick, D. W. S., Redman, T., & Maguire, S. (2013). Green human resource management: A review and research agenda: Green human resource management. *International Journal of Management Reviews*, *15*(1), 1–14. https://doi.org/10.1111/j.1468-2370.2011.00328.x

Rotaris, L., & Danielis, R. (2014). The impact of transportation demand management policies on commuting to college facilities: A case study at the University of Trieste, Italy.

Transportation Research. Part A, Policy and Practice, 67, 127–140. https://doi.org/10.1016/j.tra.2014.06.011

Sarkis, J. (2012). A boundaries and flows perspective of green supply chain management. *Supply Chain Management: An International Journal, 17*(2), 202–216. https://doi.org/10.1108/13598541211212924

Schuler, R. S., & Jackson, S. E. (1987). Linking competitive strategies with human resource management practices. *The Academy of Management Perspectives, 1*(3), 207–219. https://doi.org/10.5465/ame.1987.4275740

Schuler, R. S., & Jackson, S. E. (1987). Linking competitive strategies with human resource management practices. *The Academy of Management Perspectives, 1*(3), 207–219. https://doi.org/10.5465/ame.1987.4275740

Sharma, A. K., & Manimala, M. J. (2008). Sustainability of the Indian railways turnaround: A stage theory perspective. *SSRN Electronic Journal.* https://doi.org/10.2139/ssrn.2144044

Sharma, K. (2016). Conceptualization of green HRM and green HRM practices: Commitment to environment sustainability. *International Journal of Advanced Scientific Research and Management, 1*(8), 74–81.

Spangenberg, J. H., Fuad-Luke, A., & Blincoe, K. (2010). Design for Sustainability (DfS): the interface of sustainable production and consumption. *Journal of Cleaner Production, 18*(15), 1485–1493. https://doi.org/10.1016/j.jclepro.2010.06.002

Stappmanns, F. (2016). Sustainable Business Model Innovation: The Cases of Patagonia Inc. and Bureo Skateboards. *InImpact: The Journal of Innovation Impact, 8*(2).

Starik, M., & Rands, G. P. (1995). Weaving an integrated web: Multilevel and multisystem perspectives of ecologically sustainable organizations. *Academy of Management Review*, *20*(4), 908–935. https://doi.org/10.5465/amr.1995.9512280025

Steiber, A., & Alänge, S. (2013). A corporate system for continuous innovation: the case of Google Inc. *European Journal of Innovation Management*, *16*(2), 243–264. https://doi.org/10.1108/14601061311324566

Suwarno, S. (2022). Application of the UTAUT model for acceptance analysis of COBIT implementation in E-learning management with Microsoft Teams on distance learning in Batam City. *Khazanah Informatika Jurnal Ilmu Komputer Dan Informatika*, *8*(1), 25–33. https://doi.org/10.23917/khif.v8i1.15311

Tata Group Sustainability Reports. (n.d.). *Tata Group Sustainability Reports*.

Unilever. (2019). Unilever Annual Report and Accounts

Welinder, A. (2023). *Legitimizing sustainability talk in retail talk: The case of IKEA's sustainability journey*.

Wells, P., & Xenias, D. (2015). From 'freedom of the open road' to 'cocooning': Understanding resistance to change in personal private automobility. *Environmental Innovation and Societal Transitions*, *16*, 106–119.

Wipro Sustainability Reports. (n.d.). *Wipro Sustainability Reports*.